INTRODUCTION

Hello dear reader

As you are reading this text you are about to learn the Arabic language and Exactly learning the letters and their positions in the word

Of course, you will also learn how to write it so that you will not have a problems writing words in the Arabic language.

INFORMATION ABOUT THE ARABIC LANGUAGE

- Almost all the letters in an Arabic word are joined together like hand writing

- Arabic is read from right to left

- There are 29 letters in the Arabic alphabet

- There is no such thing as small letters vs capital letters

- All the letters in the alphabet are consonants

all The letters are on the next page

ث Thaa	ت Taa	ب Baa	أ Aleph
د Daal	خ Khaa	ح Haa	ج Jeem
س Seen	ز Zaa	ر Raa	ذ Dhaal
ط Taa	ض Daad	ص Saad	ش Sheen
ف Faa	غ Ghein	ع Ein	ظ dhaa
م Meem	ل Laam	ك Kaaf	ق Qaaf

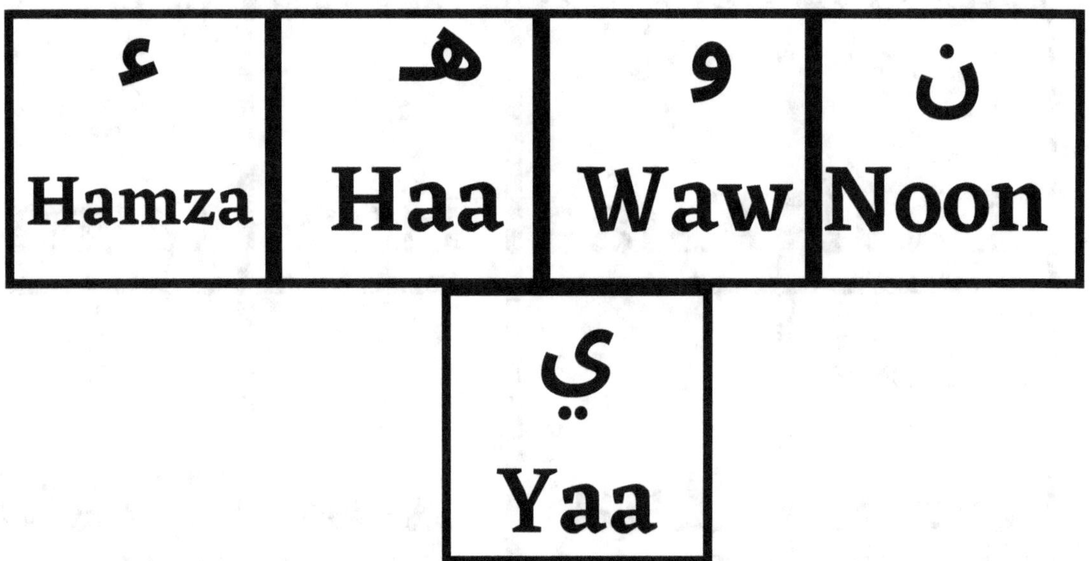

Each letter has 4 forms (which look very similar to each other)

1-when you write the letter by itself

2-when it comes in the beginning of a word

3-when it comes in the middle of a word

4-when it comes at the end of a word

The first letter of the Arabic alphabet is Aleph
This is how the Aleph looks in the four cases

end	middle	beginning of a word	by itself
ـل	ـلـ	أ	أ

On the next pages, try to rewrite each letter so that you can write it well

by itself / beginning of a word

middle / end

The next letter is Baa

Baa corresponds to the English B

This is how Baa looks in the four cases

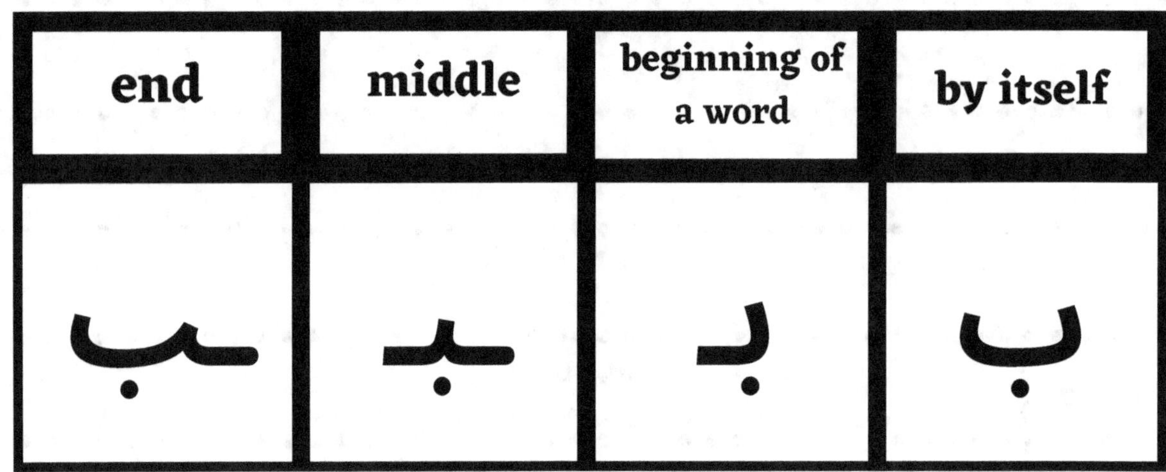

On the next pages, try to rewrite each letter so that you can write it well

by itself

beginning of a word

middle

end

ب

The next letter is Taa

Taa corresponds to the English T

This is how Taa looks in the four cases

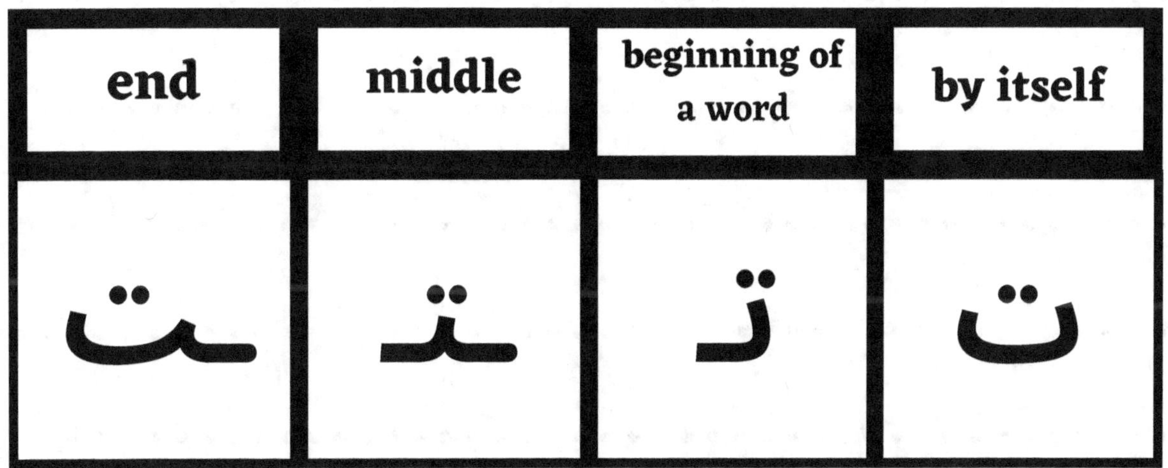

On the next pages, try to rewrite each letter so that you can write it well

by itself

ﺕ

by itself

beginning of a word

نّ

middle

end

The next letter is Thaa

Thaa corresponds to the combination TH
This is how Thaa looks in the four cases

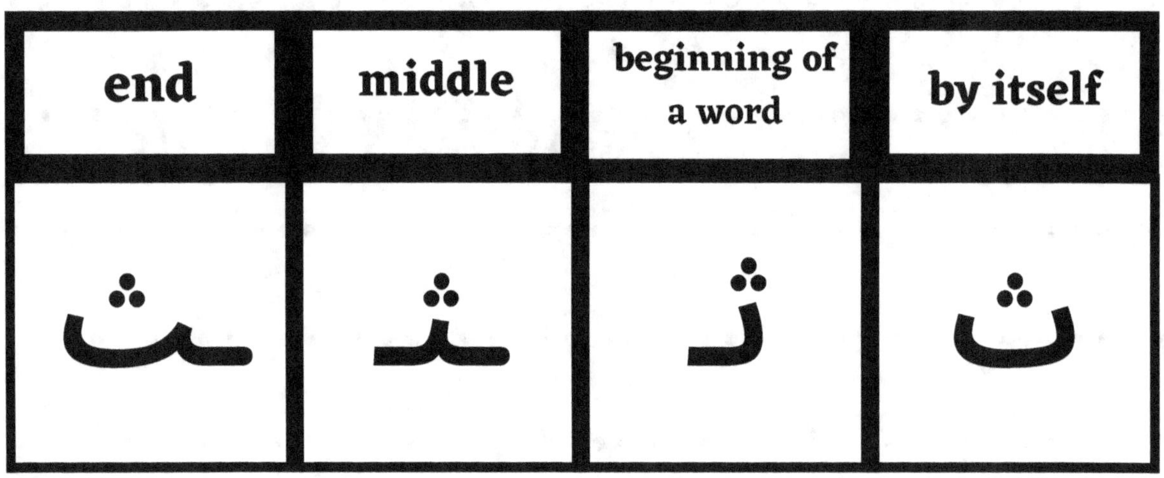

end	middle	beginning of a word	by itself
ـث	ـثـ	ثـ	ث

On the next pages, try to rewrite each letter so that you can write it well

by itself

by itself

beginning of a word

beginning of a word

middle

end

The next letter is Jeem

Jeem corresponds to the English J

This is how Jeem looks in the four cases

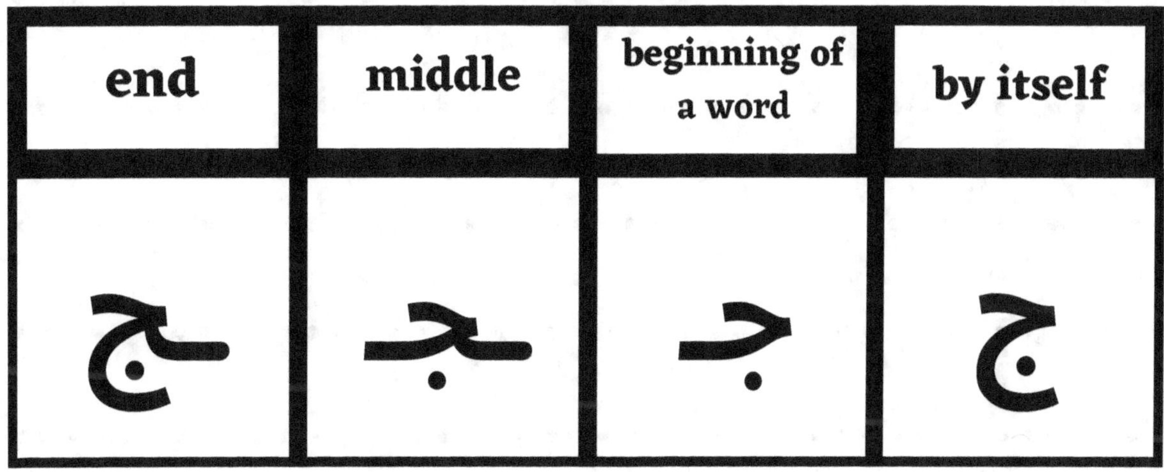

On the next pages, try to rewrite each letter so that you can write it well

by itself

beginning of a word

beginning of a word

middle

end

The next letter is Haa

Haa corresponds to the English H, but it's much more throaty

This is how Haa looks in the four cases

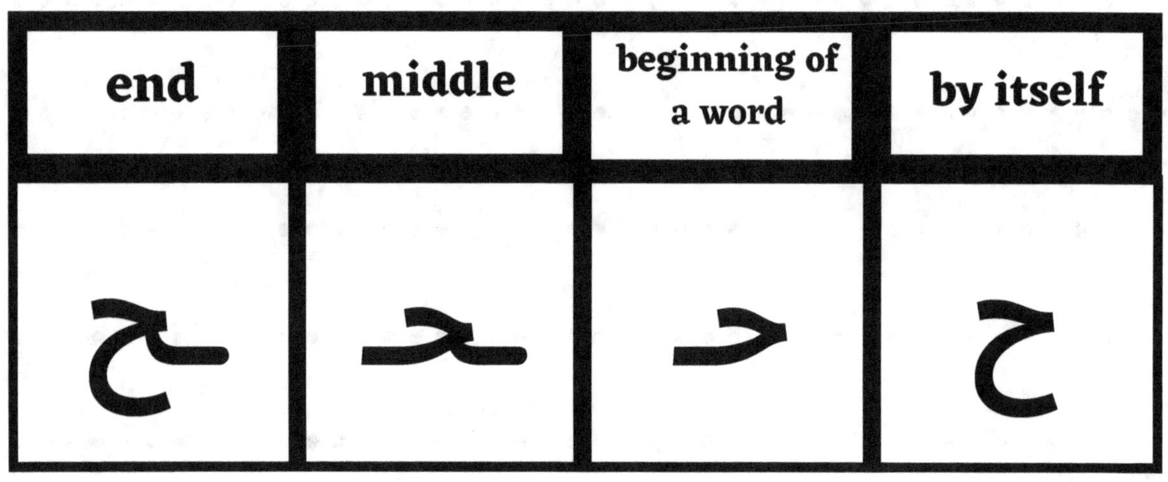

On the next pages, try to rewrite each letter so that you can write it well

by itself

beginning of a word

middle

end

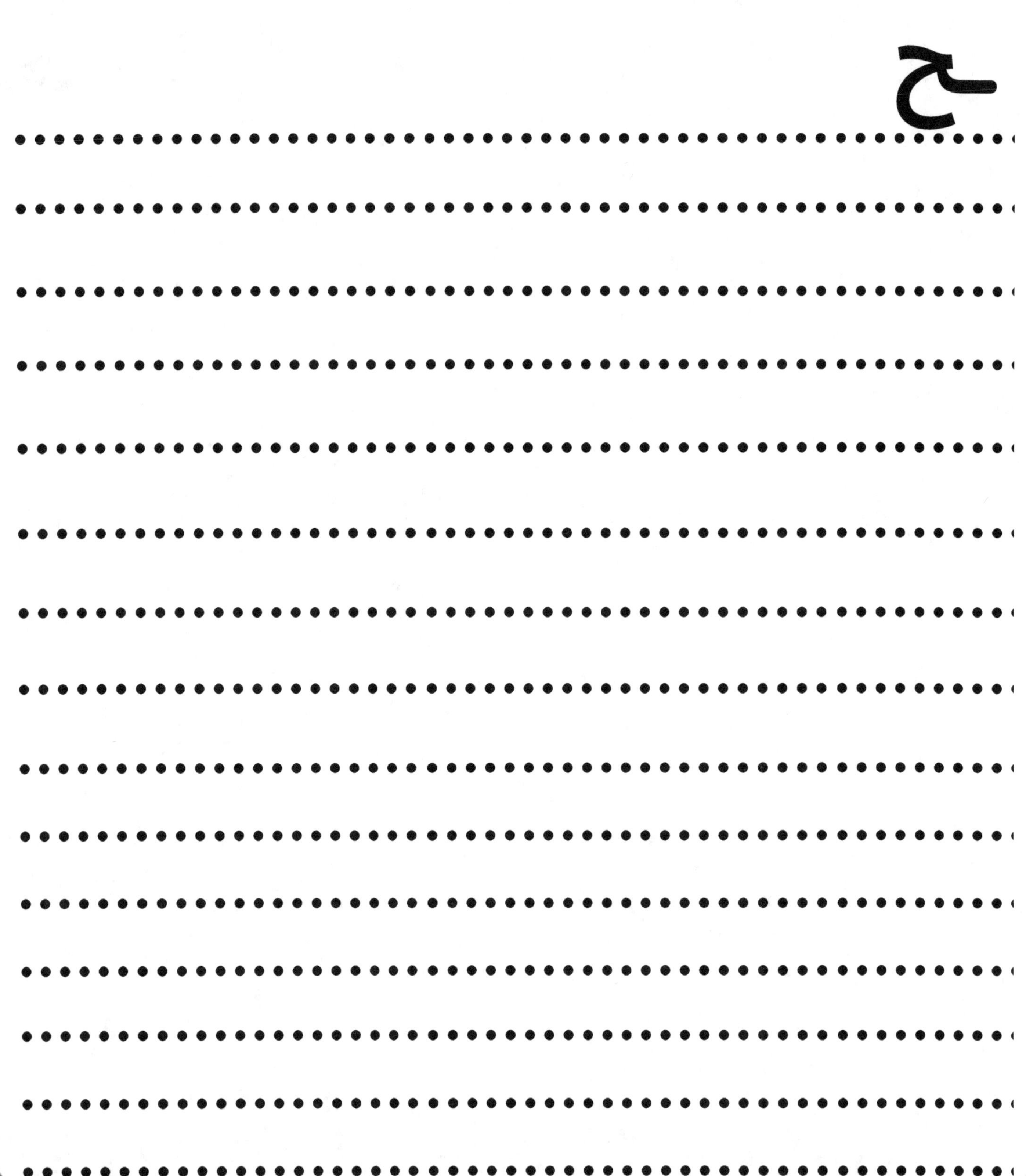

The next letter is Khaa

Khaa corresponds to the combination KH

This is how Khaa looks in the four cases

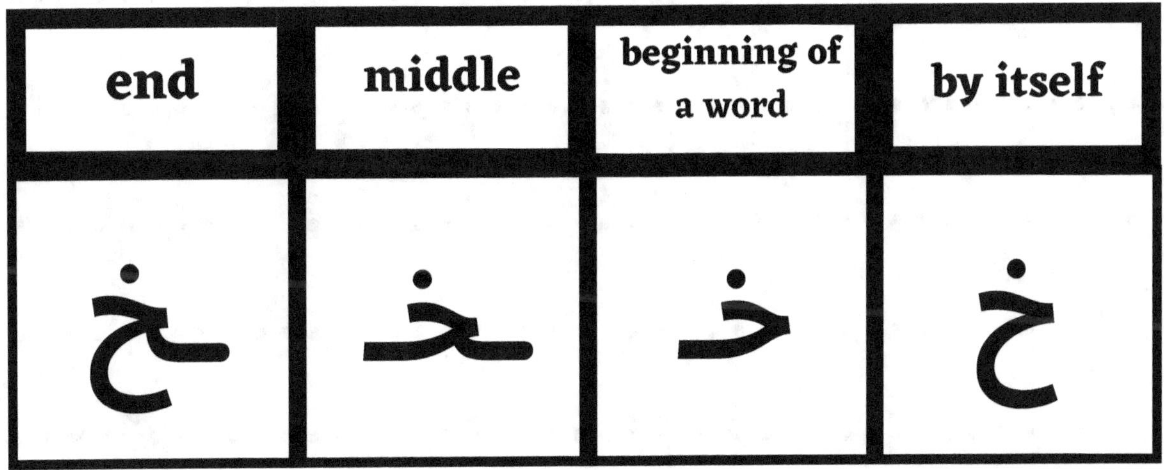

On the next pages, try to rewrite each letter so that you can write it well

by itself

خ

beginning of a word

middle

end

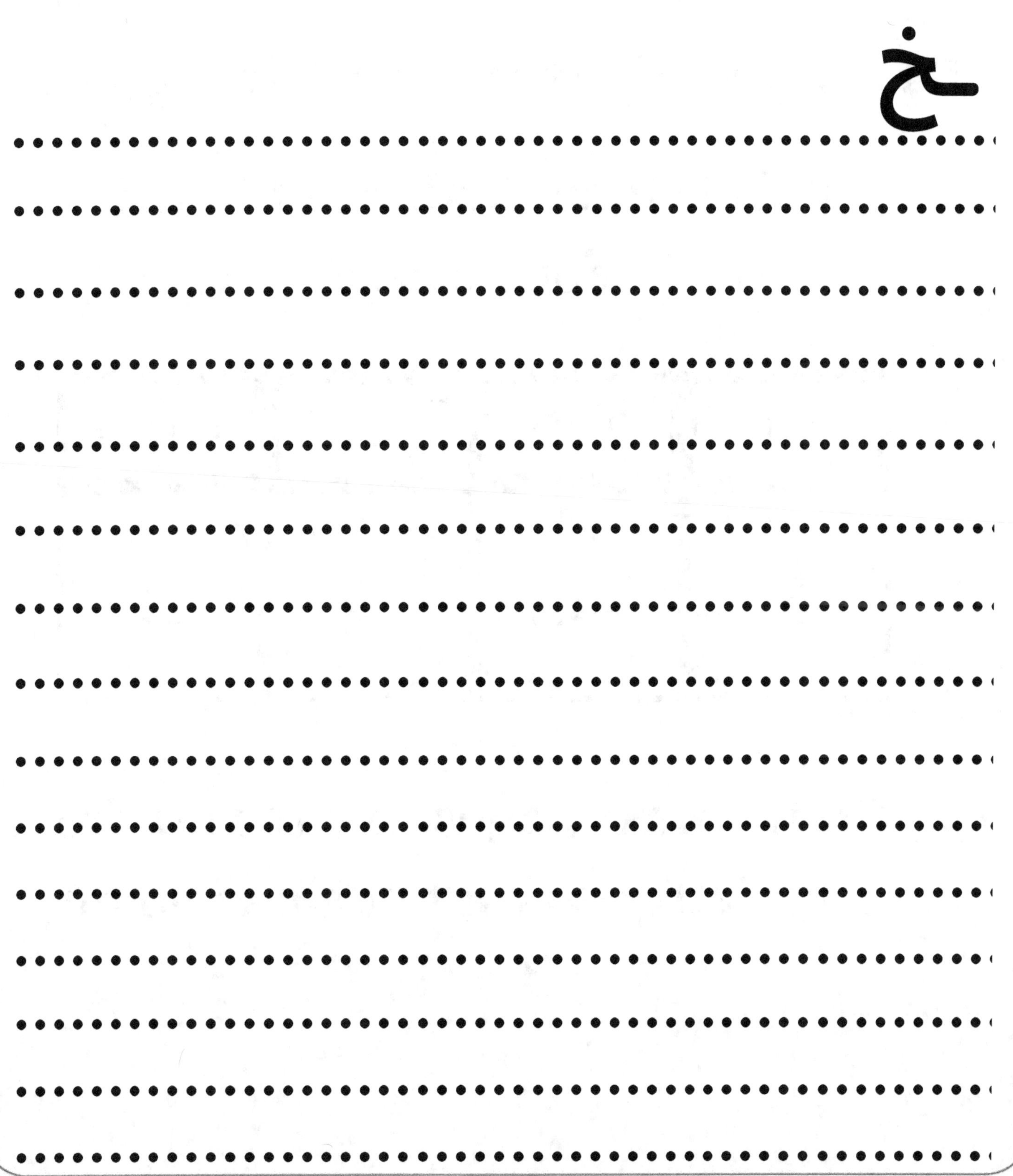

The next letter is Daal

Daal sounds like the letter D in English

This is how Daal looks in the four cases

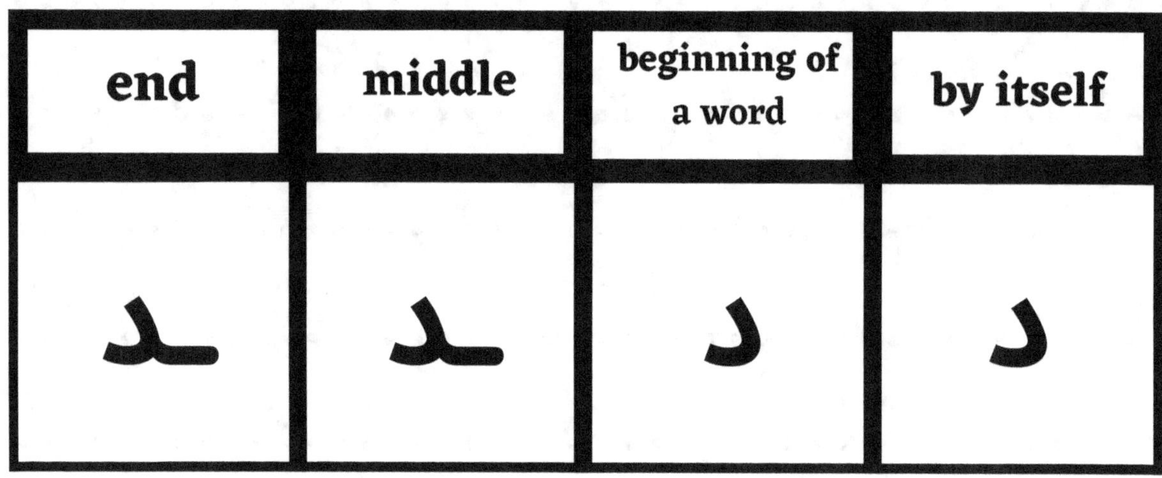

On the next pages, try to rewrite each letter so that you can write it well

by itself /beginning of a word

by itself /beginning of a word

middle /end

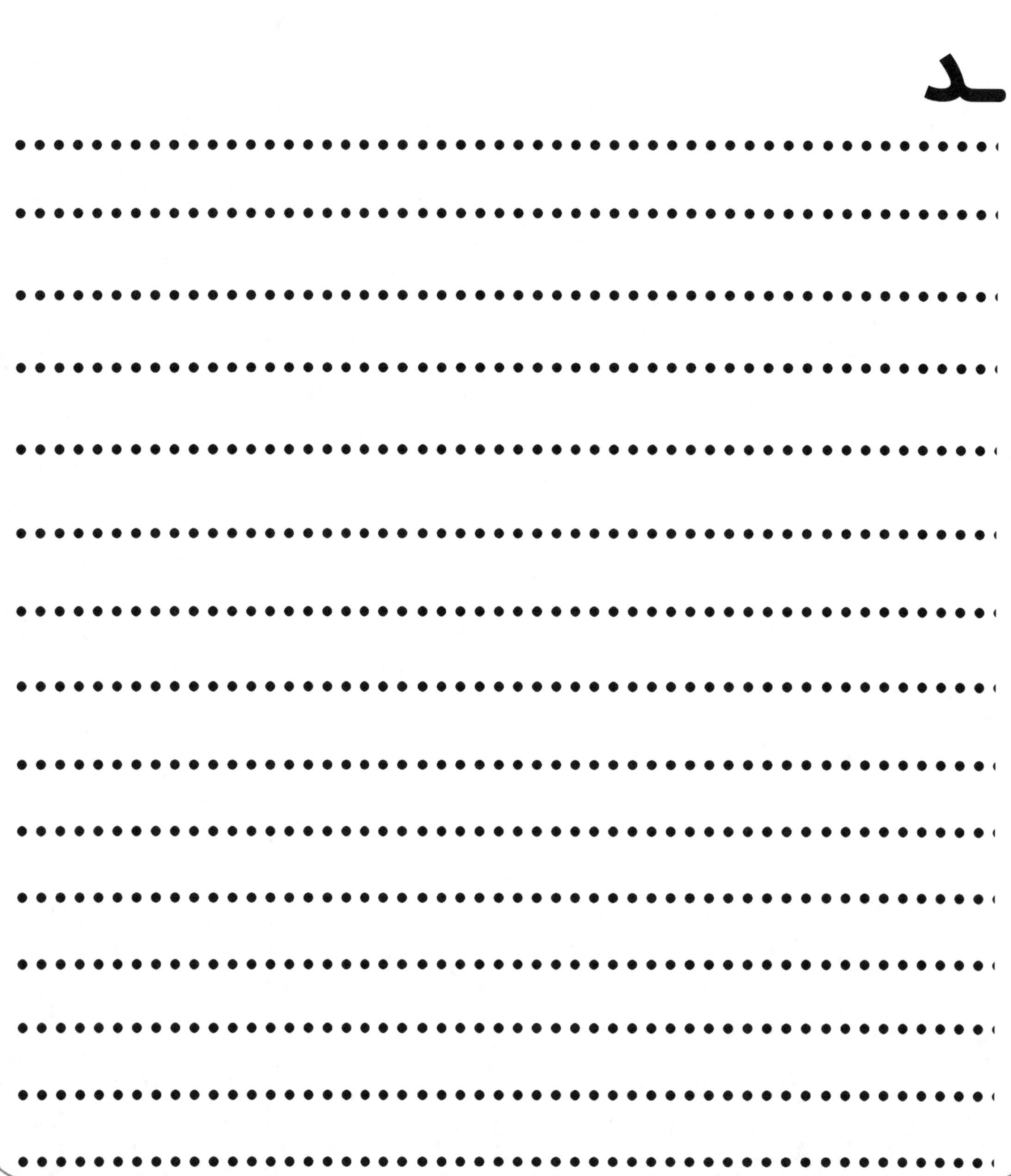

The next letter is Dhaal

Dhaal sounds like the combination TH, as in "that"

This is how Dhaal looks in the four cases

end	middle	beginning of a word	by itself
ـذ	ـذـ	ذ	ذ

On the next pages, try to rewrite each letter so that you can write it well

by itself /beginning of a word

ز

by itself /beginning of a word

middle /end

The next letter is Raa

Raa sounds like the letter R in English

This is how Raa looks in the four cases

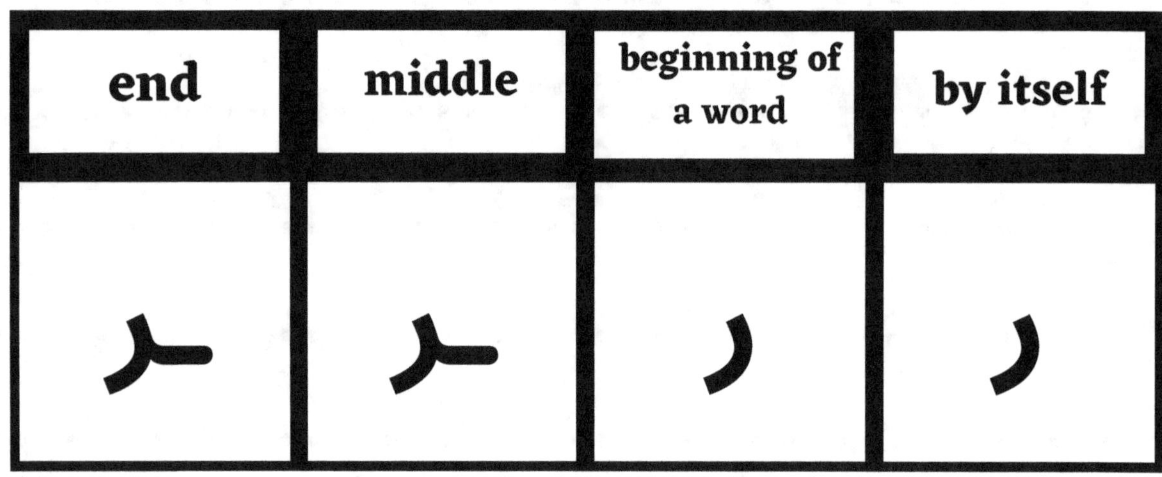

On the next pages, try to rewrite each letter so that you can write it well

by itself / beginning of a word

middle / end

The next letter is Zeiy

Zeiy sounds like the letter Z in English

This is how Zeiy looks in the four cases

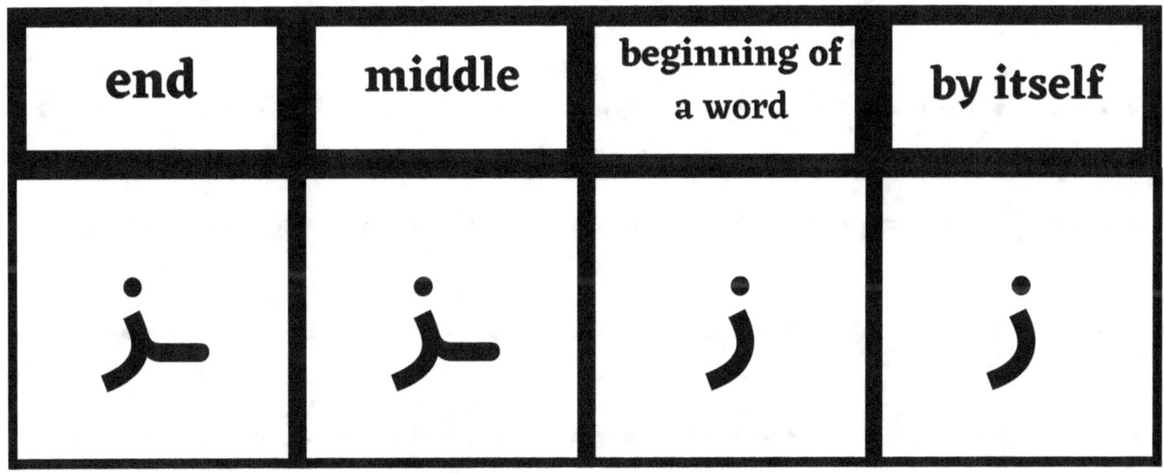

On the next pages, try to rewrite each letter so that you can write it well

by itself / beginning of a word

ز

by itself / beginning of a word

middle / end

The next letter is Seen

Seen is equivalent to the letter S

This is how Seen looks in the four cases

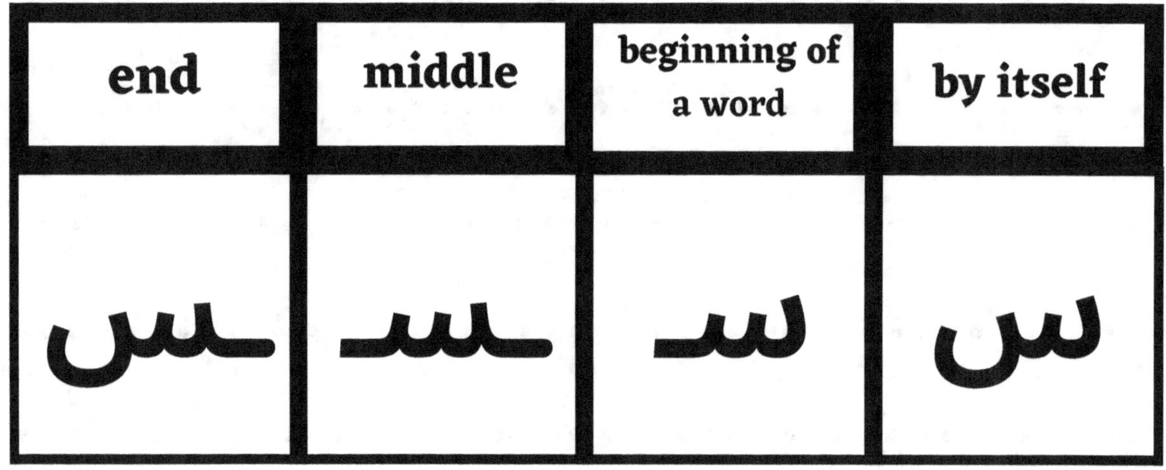

end	middle	beginning of a word	by itself
ﺲ	ﺴ	ﺳ	س

On the next pages, try to rewrite each letter so that you can write it well

by itself

 س

by itself

beginning of a word

middle

end

س

The next letter is Sheen

Sheen is equivalent to the combination SH

This is how Sheen looks in the four cases

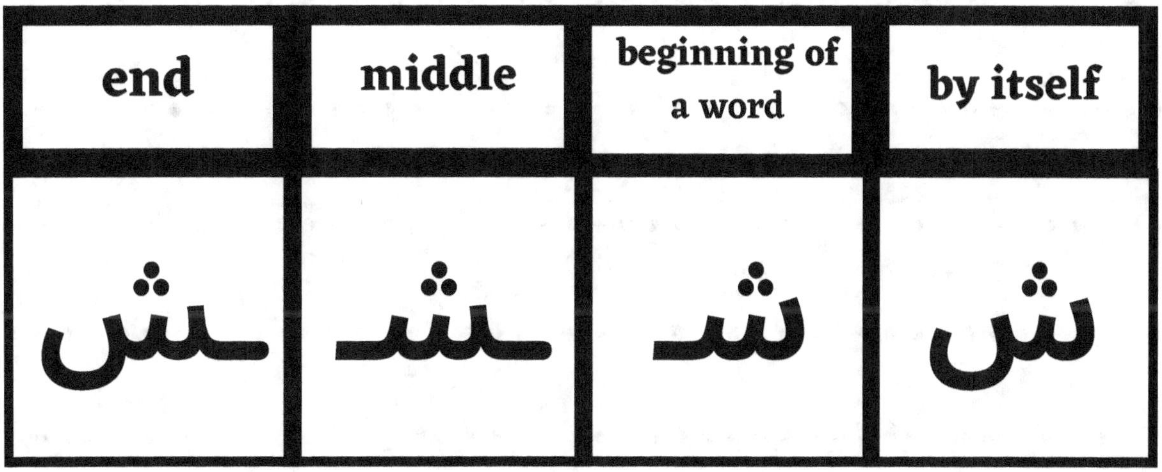

On the next pages, try to rewrite each letter so that you can write it well

by itself

ش

beginning of a word

middle

end

The next letter is Saad

Saad sounds like the letter S but it has more of a whistle
This is how Saad looks in the four cases

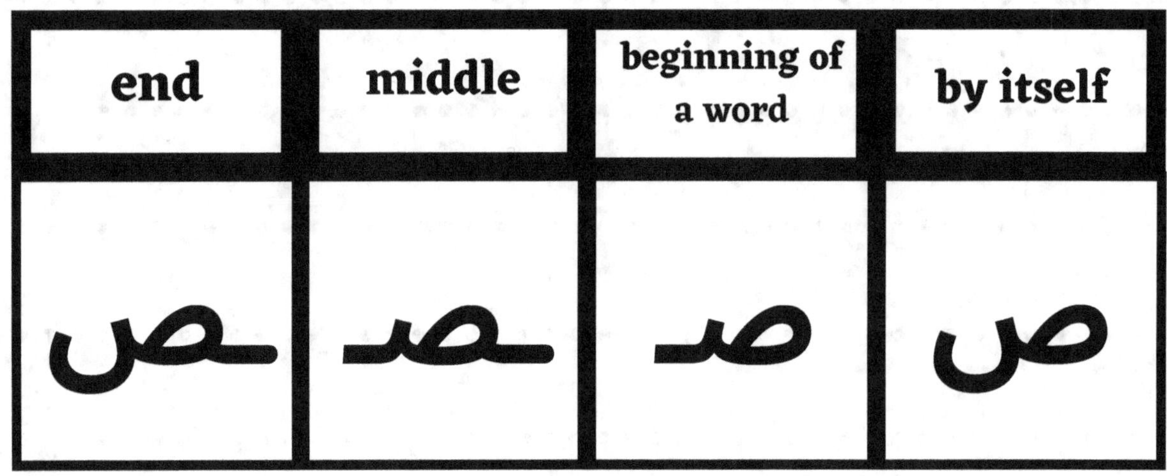

On the next pages, try to rewrite each letter so that you can write it well

by itself

beginning of a word

beginning of a word

middle

end

The next letter is Daad

Daad sounds like the letter D but much
deeper sounding
This is how Daad looks in the
four cases

end	middle	beginning of a word	by itself
ض ـض	ـضـ ـضـ	ضـ ضـ	ض ض

On the next pages, try to rewrite
each letter so that you can write
it well

by itself
ض
by itself

beginning of a word

middle

end

ض

end

The next letter is Taa

Taa sounds like the letter T but much thicker sounding This is how Taa looks in the four cases

end	middle	begining of a word	by itself
ط	ط	ط	ط

On the next pages, try to rewrite each letter so that you can write it well

by itself / beginning of a word

ط

The next letter is Dhaa

Dhaa sounds like the letter Th but more deeper sounding
This is how Dhaa looks in the four cases

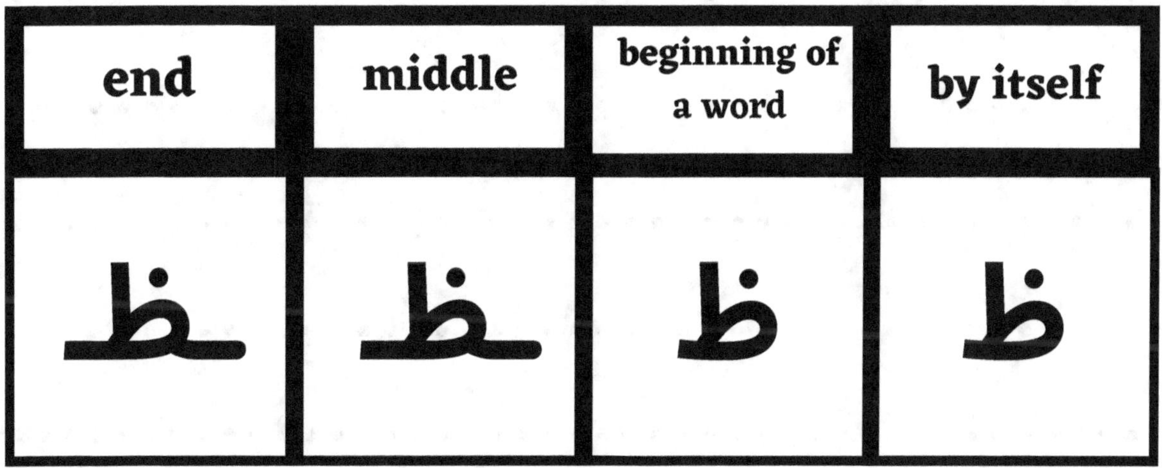

On the next pages, try to rewrite each letter so that you can write it well

by itself / beginning of a word

ظ

by itself / beginning of a word

middle / end

The next letter is Ein

Ein doesn't have an English equivalent

This is how Ein looks in the four cases

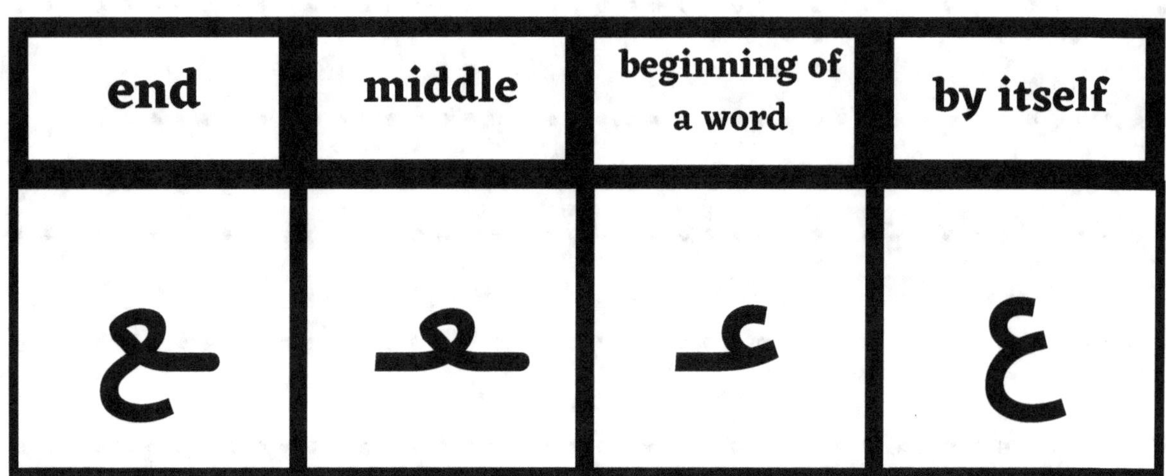

On the next pages, try to rewrite each letter so that you can write it well

by itself

beginning of a word

ﻋ

middle

end

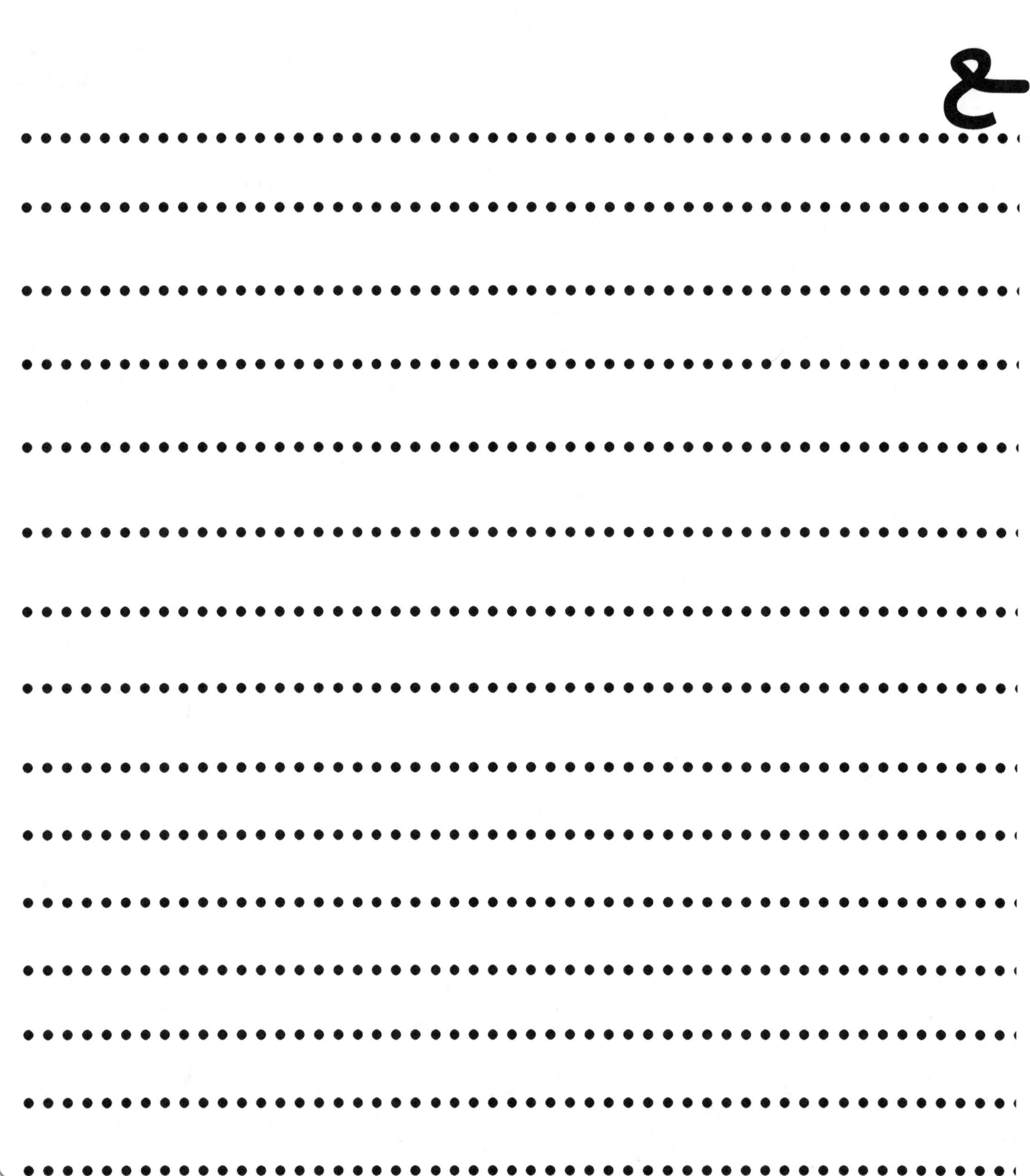

The next letter is Ghein

Ghein sounds like the combination GH

This is how Ghein looks in the four cases

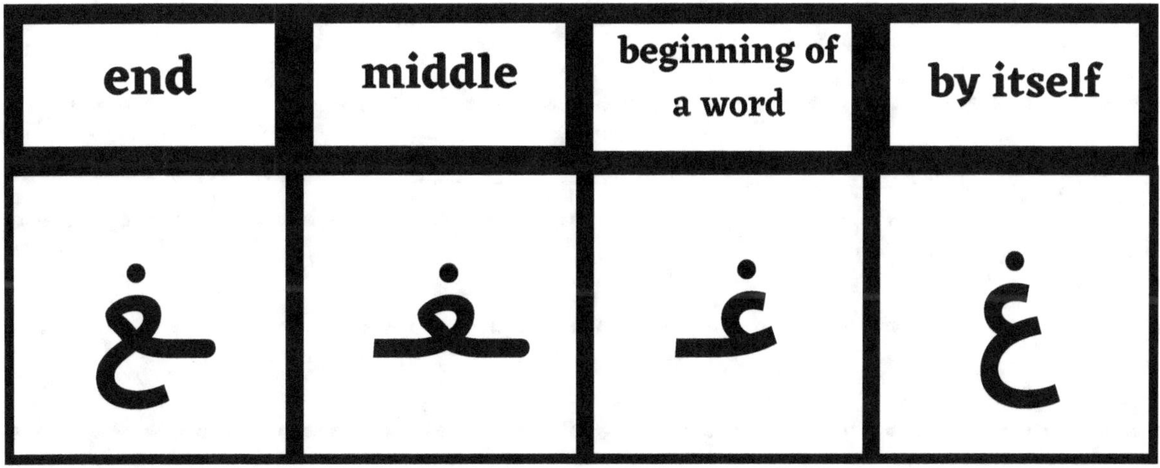

end	middle	beginning of a word	by itself
غ	ـغـ	غـ	غ

On the next pages, try to rewrite each letter so that you can write it well

by itself

غ

beginning of a word

middle

end

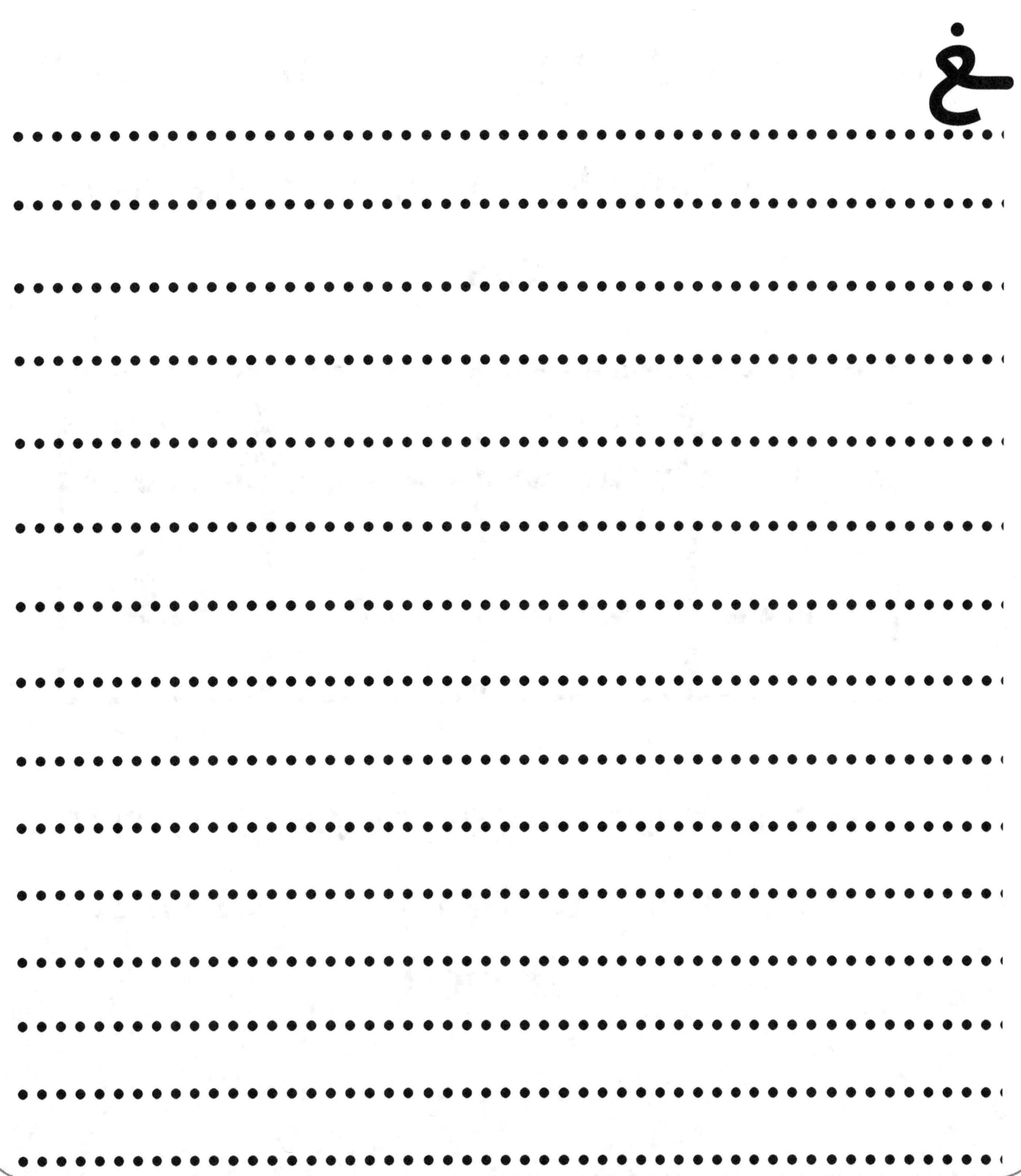

The next letter is Faa

Faa is equivalent to the English letter F

This is how Faa looks in the four cases

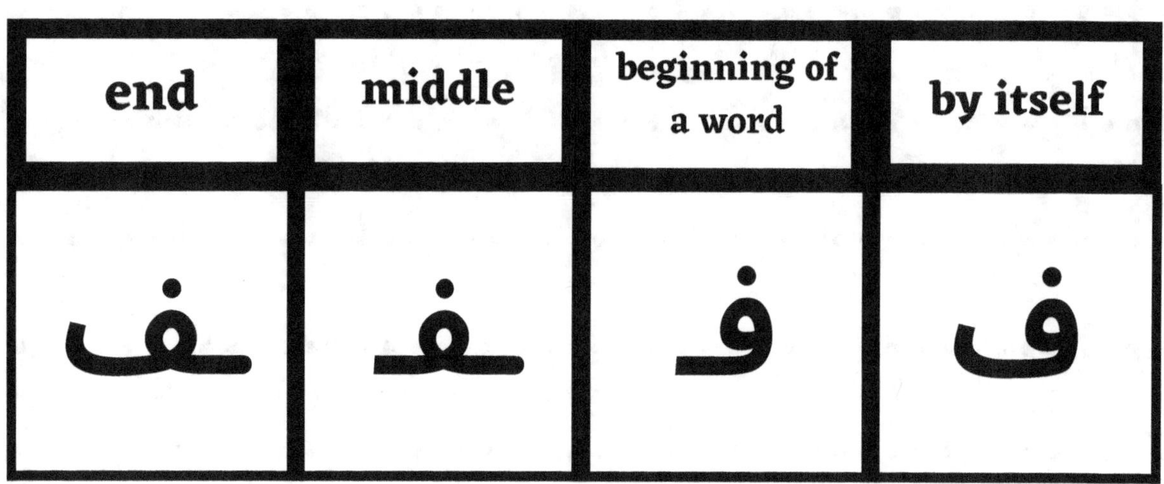

end	middle	beginning of a word	by itself
ـف	ـفـ	فـ	ف

On the next pages, try to rewrite each letter so that you can write it well

by itself

ف

by itself

beginning of a word

ف

middle

middle

end

The next letter is Qaaf

Qaaf is represented by the letter Q it sounds like K except it's more throaty

This is how Qaaf looks in the four cases

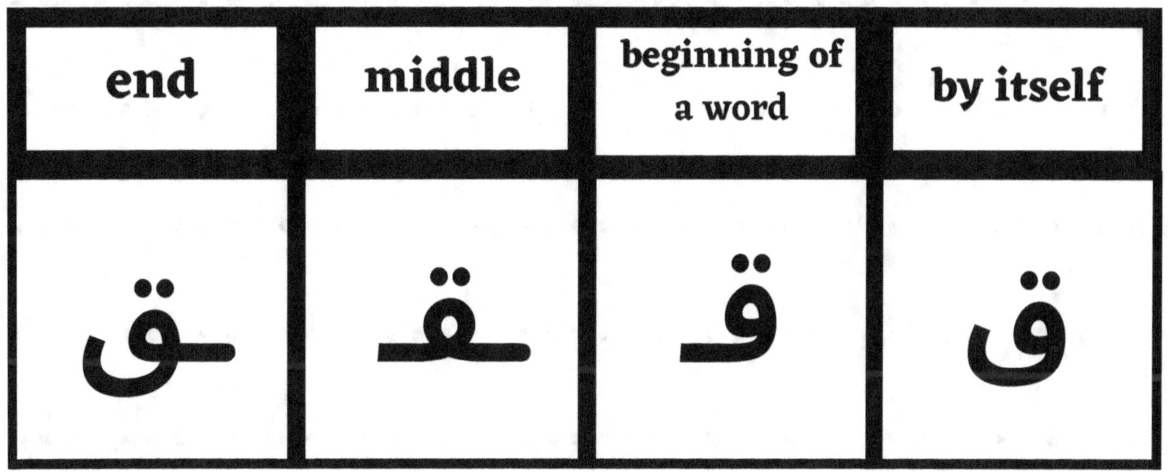

On the next pages, try to rewrite each letter so that you can write it well

by itself

ق

by itself

beginning of a word

ق

beginning of a word

middle

end

ق

The next letter is Kaaf

Kaaf is equivalent to the English letter K

This is how Kaaf looks in the four cases

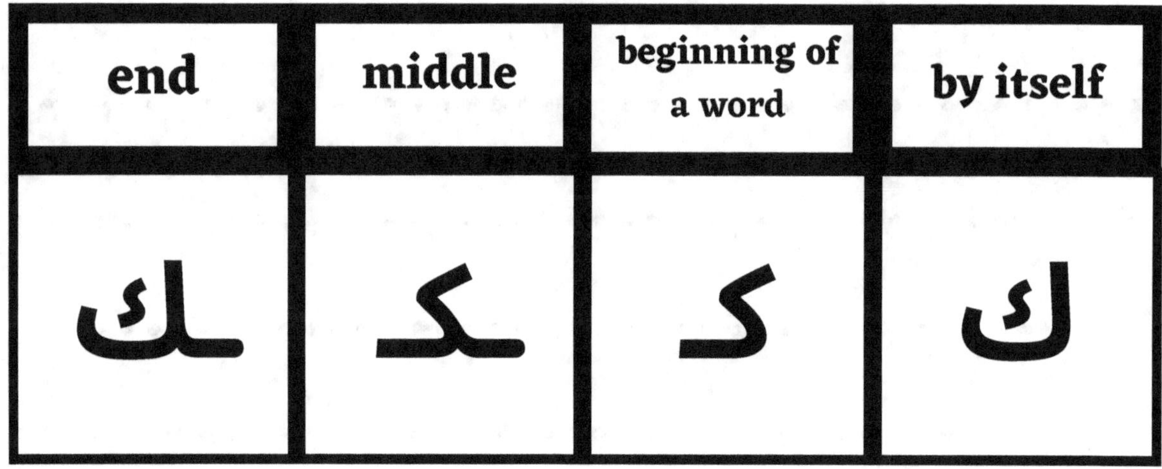

end	middle	beginning of a word	by itself
ك	ک	ک	ك

On the next pages, try to rewrite each letter so that you can write it well

by itself

ك

by itself

beginning of a word

middle

end

ـك

The next letter is Laam

Laam is equivalent to the English letter L

This is how Laam looks in the
four cases

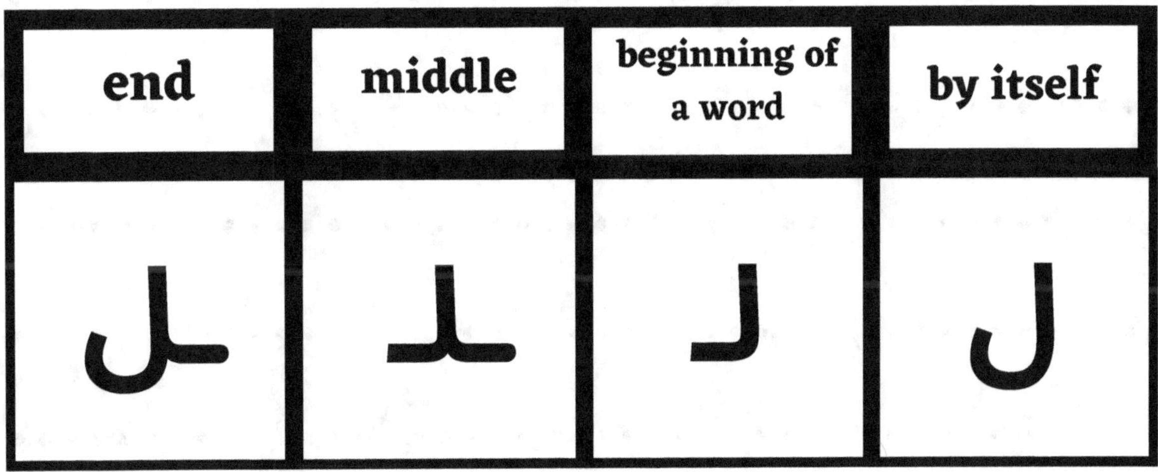

On the next pages, try to rewrite
each letter so that you can write
it well

by itself

beginning of a word

middle

end

The next letter is Meem

Meem is equivalent to the English letter M

This is how Meem looks in the four cases

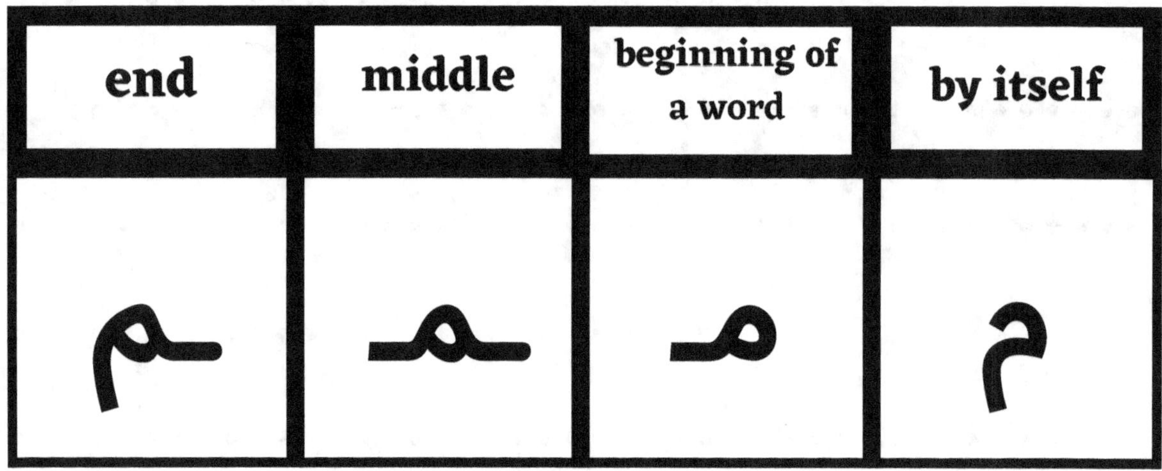

end	middle	beginning of a word	by itself
ﻢ	ﻤ	ﻣ	م

On the next pages, try to rewrite each letter so that you can write it well

by itself

beginning of a word

ﻓ

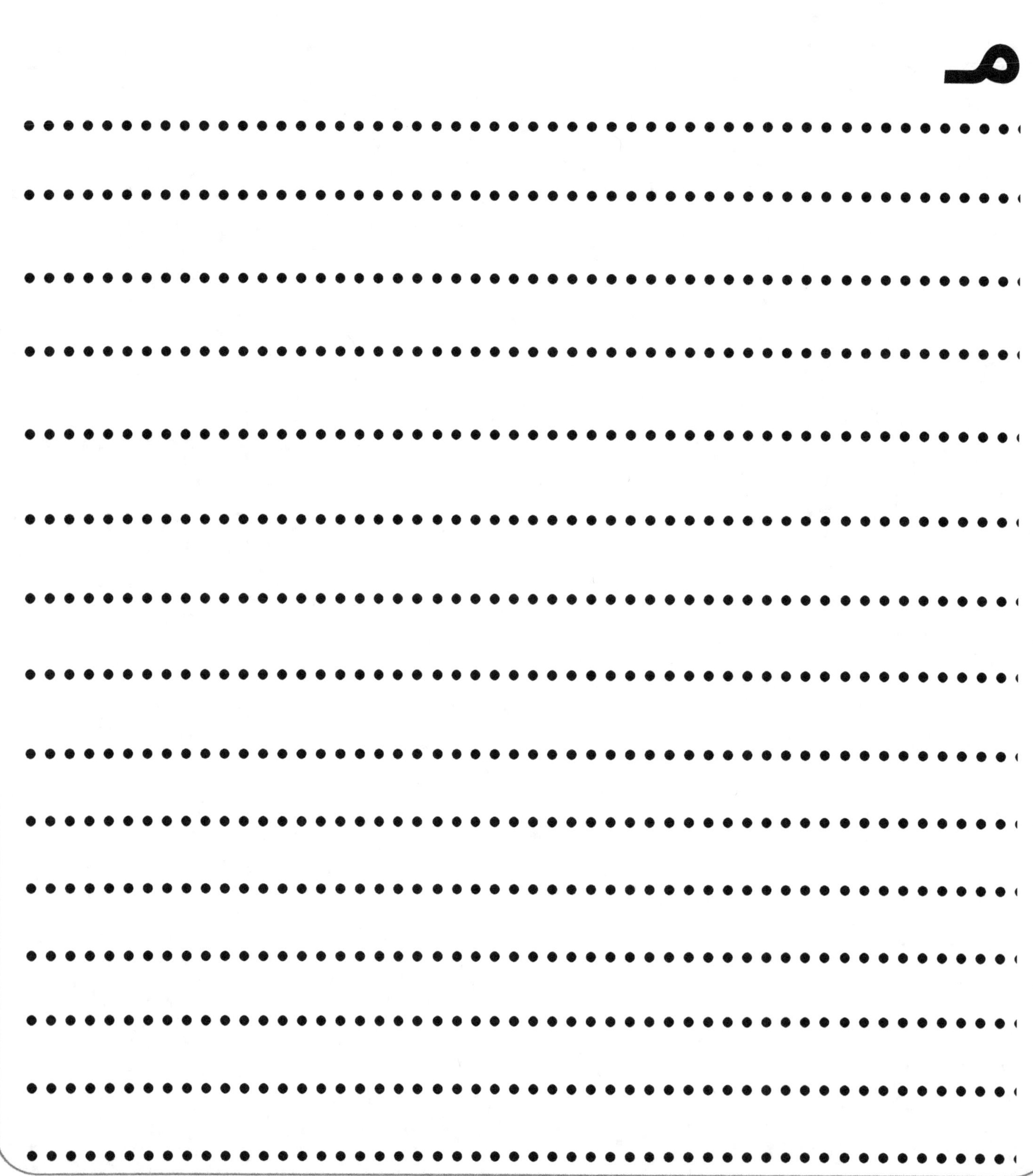

beginning of a word

middle

end

The next letter is Noon

Noon is equivalent to the English letter N

This is how Noon looks in the four cases

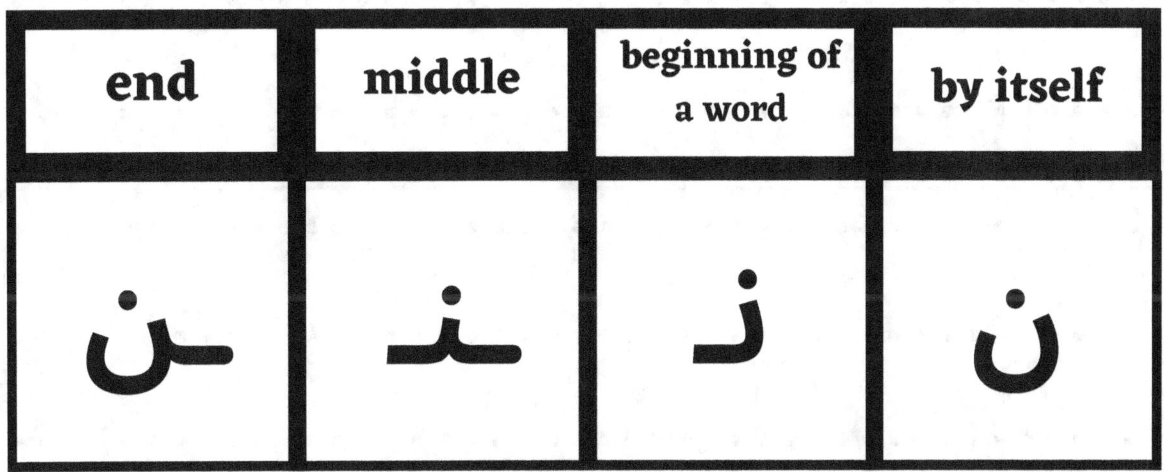

On the next pages, try to rewrite each letter so that you can write it well

by itself

by itself

beginning of a word

middle

middle

end

The next letter is Waw

Waw is equivalent to the English letter W

This is how Waw looks in the four cases

end	middle	beginning of a word	by itself
ـو	ـوـ	و	و

On the next pages, try to rewrite each letter so that you can write it well

by itself /beginning of a word

و

by itself /beginning of a word

middle / end

The next letter is Haa

Haa is equivalent to the English letter H

This is how Haa looks in the four cases

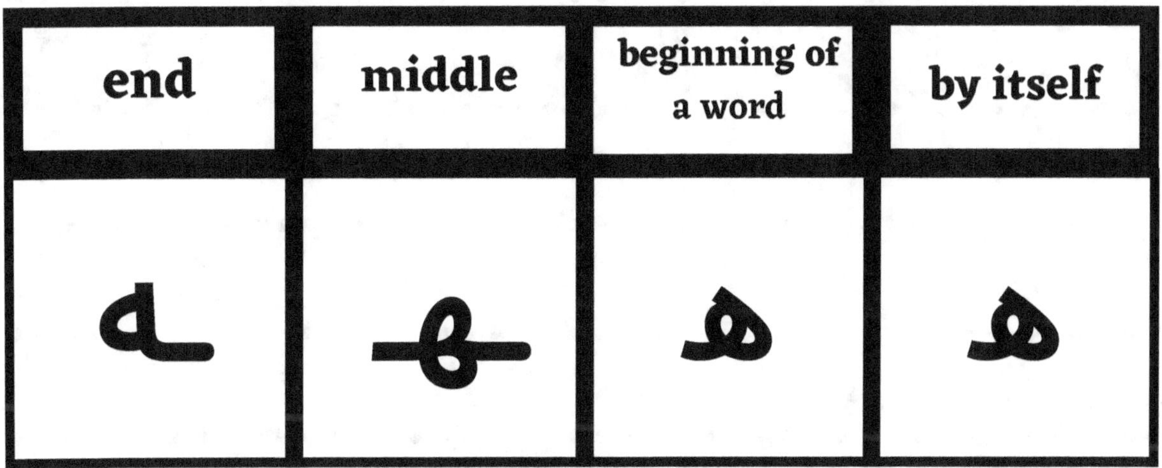

On the next pages, try to rewrite each letter so that you can write it well

by itself /beginning of a word

middle

end

The next letter is Hamza

Hamza is equivalent to the English letter A
as in "apple"
(not considered a vowel)
This is how Hamza looks in the
four cases

end	middle	beginning of a word	by itself
ئ	ئ	أ إ	ء

On the next pages, try to rewrite
each letter so that you can write
it well

by itself

ع

beginning of a word

beginning of a word

middle / end

ئ

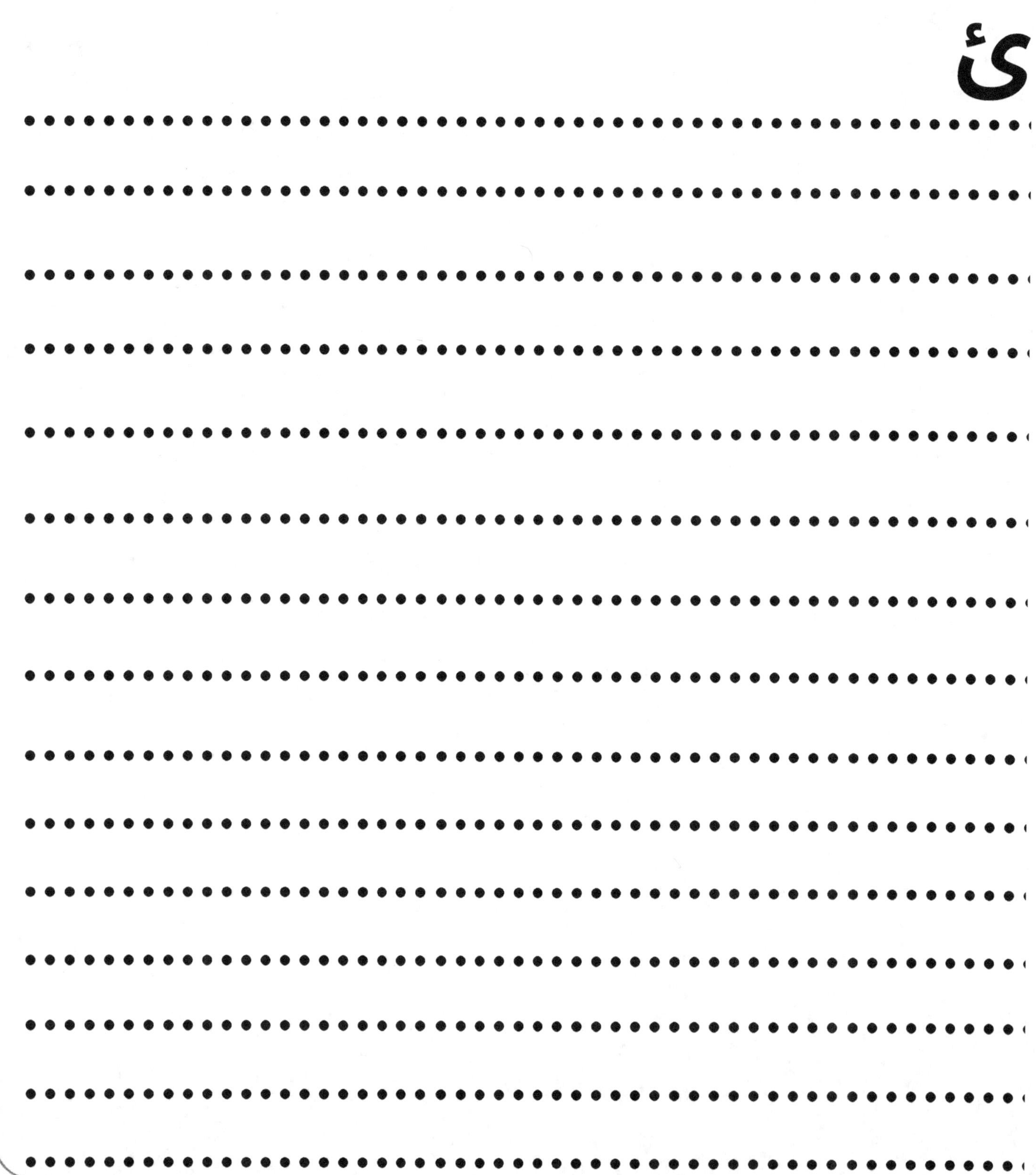

The next letter is Yaa

Yaa is equivalent to the English letter Y

This is how Yaa looks in the four cases

end	middle	beginning of a word	by itself
ي	ـيـ	يـ	ي

On the next pages, try to rewrite each letter so that you can write it well

by itself

beginning of a word

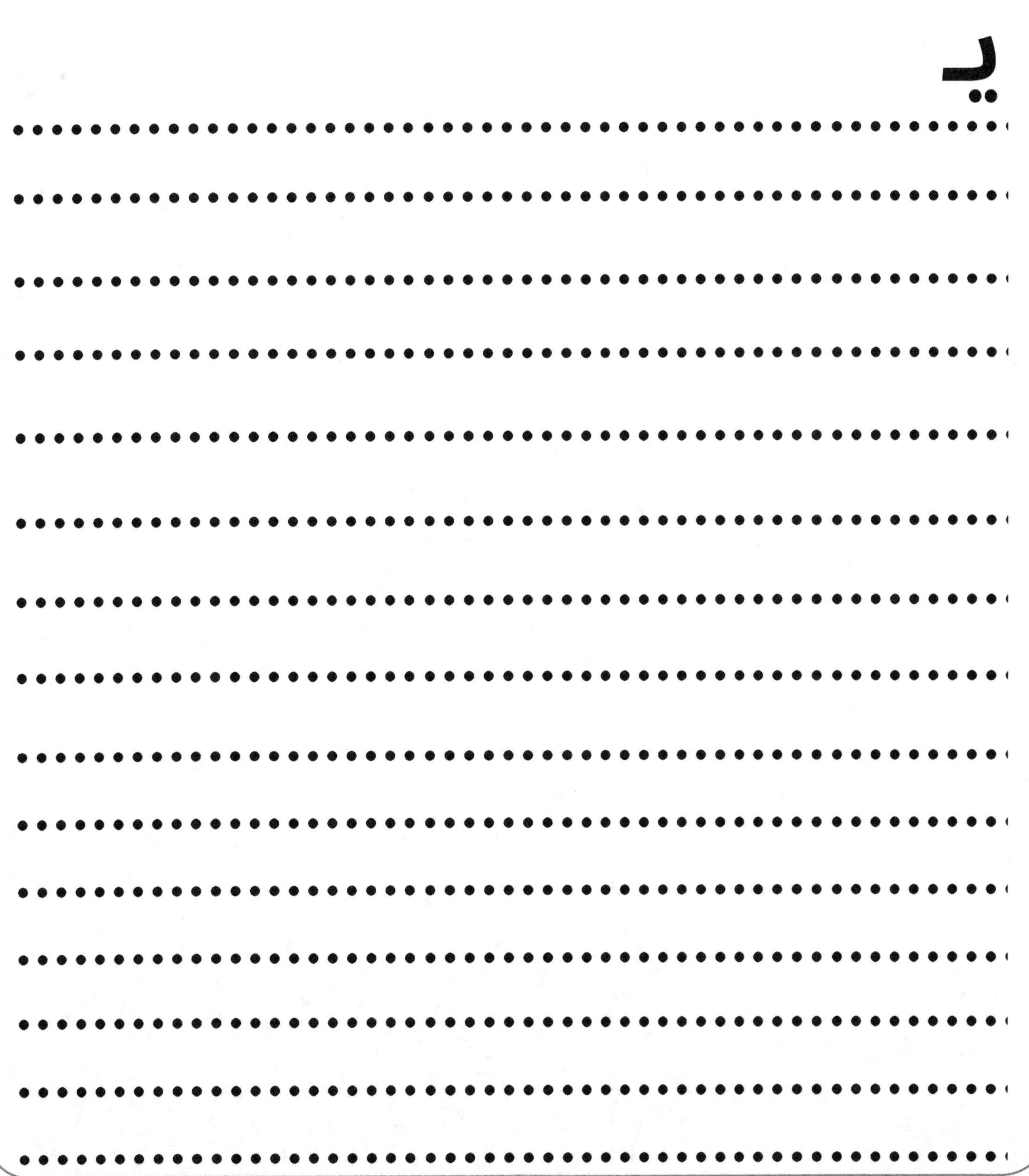

beginning of a word

middle

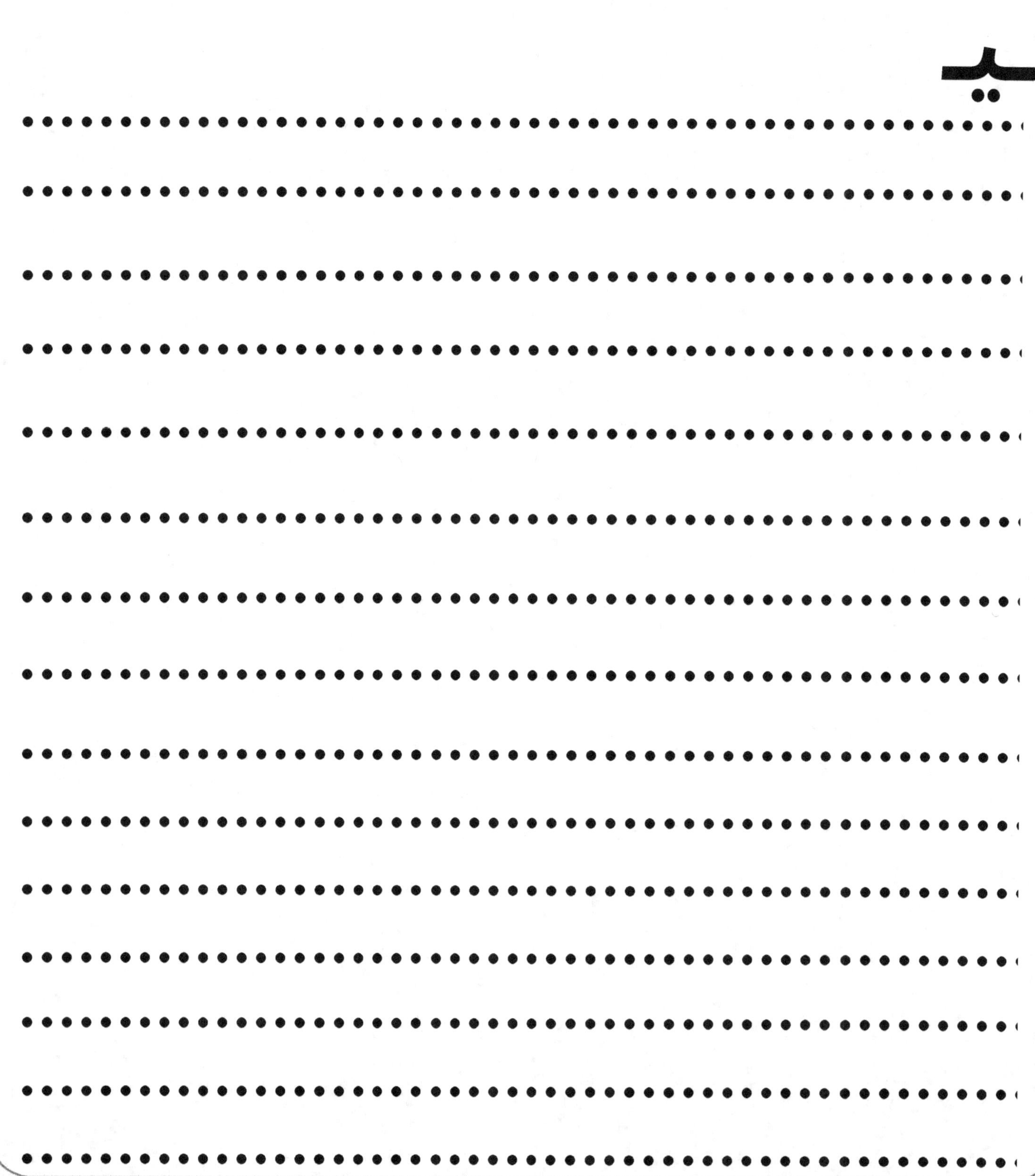

middle

end

چ

Congratulations, sir \ madam

you did well

You are now able to write all the letters of the Arabic alphabet in their correct position in the word without facing any problem